The Amazing Geography of the West

by Vana Dougias

PEARSON

Scott Foresman

Editorial Offices: Glenview, Illinois • Parsippany, New Jersey • New York, New York
Sales Offices: Needham, Massachusetts • Duluth, Georgia • Glenview, Illinois
Coppell, Texas • Ontario, California • Mesa, Arizona

ISBN: 0-328-13425-2

7 8 9 10 V0G1 14 13 12 11 10 09 08

The western United States has a lot to offer to someone looking for adventure. If you have ever visited California, Washington, or other western states, then you may have seen some of the most **impressive** sights and spots anywhere. Mount Rainier, shown below, is just one of these. When you travel out West, you will find some of the highest mountains and the lowest valleys in the United States. You will also see some of the most beautiful, ancient geographical wonders in the world.

Mount Rainier is one of our beautiful natural resources.

One of the best ways to explore the amazing land forms of the western United States is to visit a national park. National parks are areas that have been set aside. They **preserve** the natural landforms and protect the precious wildlife found there.

In 1872 Yellowstone National Park became the world's first national park. It covers parts of Wyoming, Idaho, and Montana. Eighteen years later, in 1890, Yosemite National Park was established in California. Soon, many other parks were created in the United States.

Waterfall (left) and gold mine site (right) at Yellowstone National Park in Wyoming

There is a lot to learn about our nation's national parks. Yellowstone covers more than two million acres. It's no mystery where Yellowstone got its name. Much of the rock there is yellowish sandstone.

Yellowstone is famous for its geysers, such as the one called Old Faithful. Geysers happen when water is heated by volcanic material under Earth's surface. Sometimes the water gets so hot that steam pressure is created. This causes the heated water to gush up out of the ground.

Old Faithful is the most famous geyser in Yellowstone. It got its name because of its predictable eruptions.

Yellowstone is home to forests, rivers, mountains, a canyon, and many kinds of wildlife. Many different animal **species** live in Yellowstone. Among them are grizzly bears, bison, moose, and elk. In fact, Yellowstone protects a large ecosystem, or environment, that includes animals such as coyotes, wolverines, and mountain lions. Park safety officials warn guests to keep a safe distance as they watch the wildlife, because wild animals can be dangerous.

Yellowstone National Park during the spring

Elk

Coyote

In addition to Yellowstone, there are many other places in the western United States that are unique. There are several mountain ranges in the western part of the country. The Rocky Mountains stretch all the way from Mexico, through the United States, and into Canada and Alaska. They form the geographical boundary between the midwestern and western regions of the United States. Pikes Peak, one of the mountains in the Colorado Rockies, is a popular tourist attraction. It has an interesting history.

Life in the Rocky Mountains

Mountain goats

Lime swallowtail

Pikes Peak is named for explorer Zebulon Pike. He tried to climb the great mountain in 1806. Pike and his fellow climbers were unsuccessful. A snowstorm forced them to turn back. Since then, many people have visited and climbed Pikes Peak. Pikes Peak became an important landmark for wagon trains heading west in search of gold and land in the 1850s. In 1893, Katharine Lee Bates, a teacher from Massachusetts, was amazed by the view from the top of Pikes Peak. It inspired her to write the lyrics to the song "America the Beautiful."

Ride up Pikes Peak in a car or on the cog railway.

Zebulon Pike

Pikes Peak is not the only famous mountain in the western United States. The West is home to some of the highest peaks in the world. One of the most impressive is Mount Rainier in Washington State. It is part of a mountain range called the Cascades. Although it is covered in layers of snow and ice, Mount Rainier is actually a 14,410-foot volcano! Two million people visit Mount Rainier each year. Some visitors like to climb, hike, or ski its **slopes.** Others go to see the beautiful wildflowers that grow in the meadows near its base.

Mount Rainier

Mount St. Helens is another volcano in the Cascade Range. It is also located in Washington. Mount Rainier and Mount St. Helens are part of a group of volcanoes called the Pacific Ring of Fire. These volcanoes got their name because they are close to the Pacific Ocean and they form the rough outline of a ring. Many volcanoes in the ring are active. On the morning of May 18, 1980, Mount St. Helens erupted. An earthquake triggered the eruption, which lasted nine hours. The volcano released so much ash into the sky that the day seemed to turn into night.

Mount St. Helens

Before its eruption in 1980, Mount St. Helens was known for its beautiful peak. After the eruption, Mount St. Helens looked very different. Although the mountain is still a beautiful sight, it no longer has its famous peak. The earthquake that caused the volcano to erupt also caused the north side of the mountain to collapse and slide down into the surrounding **wilderness.** An avalanche of rock and ash covered much of the forest and wildlife at the base of the mountain.

Steam, lava, and ash from Mount St. Helens

Clouds of ash from Mount St. Helens in Yakima, Washington

California is an exciting state to visit, especially for someone with an interest in land, rocks, and nature. Many earthquakes have occurred along the San Andreas Fault in California.

A fault is a fracture in Earth's crust. These are the areas where most earthquakes take place. An earthquake is a sudden shaking of Earth's surface. Did you know that minor earthquakes happen on Earth every day? Most quakes are so minor that they cause no damage, but some earthquakes are very dangerous.

There have been some major earthquakes along the San Andreas Fault, shown below. Many steps are taken to ensure the safety of people who live near fault lines. Buildings are made with special materials that help prevent damage if an earthquake occurs. People who live in these areas learn what to do to stay safe in an earthquake.

San Andreas Fault

One of the most interesting places to visit in California is Yosemite National Park. As we learned earlier, Yosemite became a national park in 1890. It was one of the first national parks ever created in the world, and it remains one of the most popular places for nature lovers to visit. More than 3.5 million people visit Yosemite every year.

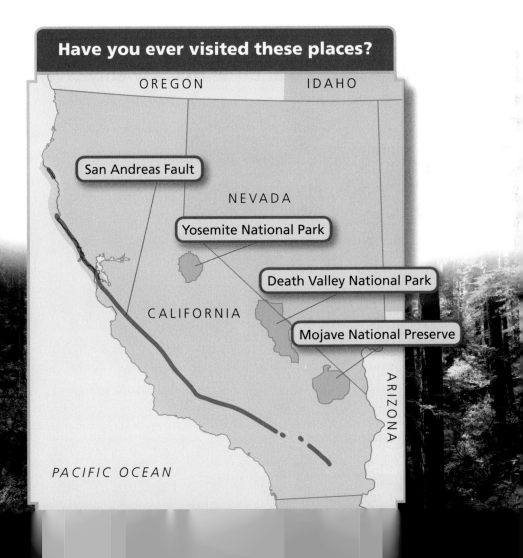

Have you ever visited these places?

Yosemite is a national treasure for many reasons. The park is located in the Sierra Nevada and offers many great views. A walk along one of the park's many trails may lead to cliffs, waterfalls, streams, and meadows.

Someone who visits Yosemite will not want to miss seeing the ancient giant sequoia trees that live in its forests. Giant sequoias are the world's largest living things! Inside Yosemite, in an area called Mariposa Grove, visitors can see these giant sequoias. In this grove is a sequoia called the Grizzly Giant. This tree is twenty-seven hundred years old!

A sequoia pine cone and bark from a sequoia tree

Another interesting place in California is the world-famous Death Valley. Death Valley is located just north of the Mojave Desert near the border between California and Nevada. It is one of the hottest places on Earth! During the summer, temperatures often rise to 120°F. Death Valley is also the lowest point in the Western Hemisphere. It is 282 feet below sea level. Despite the heat and low altitude, is a beautiful place filled with colorful rock formations, sand dunes, and desert plants.

The best way to explore the exotic beauty of Death Valley is to visit Death Valley National Park. The park is a little bigger than Death Valley itself. For people who like reptiles, this is the place to go. Visitors might see a rare species, such as the desert tortoise or the desert iguana.

A close look at cracked, dry dirt from Death Valley

There is no doubt that California has many fascinating places to visit, but Alaska and Hawaii are also two of the most beautiful and unusual parts of the United States. For someone interested in becoming a **naturalist,** Alaska and Hawaii are perfect places to begin nature studies.

Alaska is the largest U.S. state. It is home to North America's highest mountain. Mount McKinley, 20,320 feet high, rises majestically in Alaska's Denali National Park and Preserve.

Mountains and wildlife

Grizzly bear cub

Caribou

Mount McKinley is part of the Alaska Range, a magnificent group of mountains and large glaciers. The movement of each **glacier** helped to form the dramatic landscape of Denali many thousands of years ago.

Denali National Park is a nature and wildlife refuge that covers more than six million acres of land. Grizzly bears, wolves, and caribou are just a few of the animals that live in Denali all year. Many bird species also live in Denali during part of the year.

Hawaii is a state with an amazing story. The state of Hawaii is made up of many islands. The Hawaiian Islands were formed by erupting volcanoes. The largest island is called Hawaii. Two enormous volcanoes on the big island of Hawaii are still active. Kilauea and Mauna Loa add land to the island of Hawaii when lava oozes out, slides down their slopes, and cools.

Mauna Loa is actually the biggest mountain in the world! If you measure Mauna Loa's height from its base at the bottom of the sea to its very top, it is about thirty thousand feet tall! That's about a thousand feet taller than Mount Everest.

Lava rocks from Kilauea volcano

Steam rising from Kilauea

The western United States is full of many geographical wonders and wildlife preserves. It is a great place to observe the habitats of many plants and animals. Thousands of years of volcanic eruptions, earthquakes, and the movement of glaciers have made amazing land formations. The beauty of the American West is just one example of why conservation of nature is so important. If we do not take care of the natural world, we could lose all the wonderful things that nature has to offer.

The Rocky Mountains in Colorado

Glossary

glacier *n.* a great mass of ice moving very slowly down a mountain, along a valley, or over a land area.

impressive *adj.* able to have a strong effect on the mind or feelings; able to influence deeply.

naturalist *n.* person who makes a study of living things.

preserve *v.* to keep from harm or change; keep safe; protect.

slopes *n.* lines, surfaces, land, etc., that goes up or down at an angle.

species *n.* a set of related living things that all have certain characteristics.

wilderness *n.* a wild uncultivated region with few or no people living in it.